THE FLYER FLEW!
The Invention of the Airplane

by **Lee Sullivan Hill**   illustrations by **Craig Orback**

On My Own

SCIENCE

M   Millbrook Press Minneapolis

Millbrook Press
A division of Lerner Publishing Group
241 First Avenue North
Minneapolis, MN 55401 U.S.A

Website address: www.lernerbooks.com

Library of Congress Cataloging-in-Publication Data

Hill, Lee Sullivan, 1958–
    The Flyer flew! : the invention of the airplane / by Lee Sullivan Hill ; illustrations by
Craig Orback.
        p. cm. — (On my own science)
    Includes bibliographical references.
    ISBN-13 : 978-1-57505-758-3 (lib. bdg. : alk. paper)
    ISBN-10 : 1-57505-758-1 (lib. bdg. : alk. paper)
    1. Wright, Orville, 1871-1948—Juvenile literature. 2. Wright, Wilbur, 1867-1912—
Juvenile literature. 3. Aeronautics—United States—History—Juvenile literature. 4.
Wright Flyer (Airplane)—Juvenile
literature. I. Orback, Craig. ill. II. Title. III. Series.
TL540.W7H538 2006
629.13'0092'27—dc22   2004022731

Manufactured in the United States of America
1 2 3 4 5 6 – JR – 11 10 09 08 07 06

The Problem

Dayton, Ohio, September 1892

Wilbur and Orville Wright pedaled
toward home.
The brothers flew downhill
on their bikes.
Watch out!
Orville veered around a wagon.

It was a close call.

But the brothers loved to ride fast.

Bicycles were new in the 1890s.

Wilbur and Orville liked them so much,

they opened a bicycle shop.

The Wright brothers liked other new
inventions too.
They read about a German flyer named
Otto Lilienthal.
He built flying machines called gliders.
Gliders weren't powered by engines.
They flew on the wind.
Lilienthal flew his gliders from a hill.
He controlled them by leaning his body
from side to side.
But this did not work very well.
Lilienthal crashed and died.
Wilbur and Orville were sad.
But they were also curious.
Why had Lilienthal crashed?
Was there a better way
to control a glider?

The brothers liked challenges.

They wanted to know more about flying.

First, the brothers read.

They learned how air could lift a glider.

Air is always pushing on objects.

This is called air pressure.

Air pressure changes when it
flows past a curved wing.

The air under the wing pushes up harder
than the air on top pushes down.

The difference between the air pushing up
and the air pushing down is called lift.

Lift makes an aircraft fly.

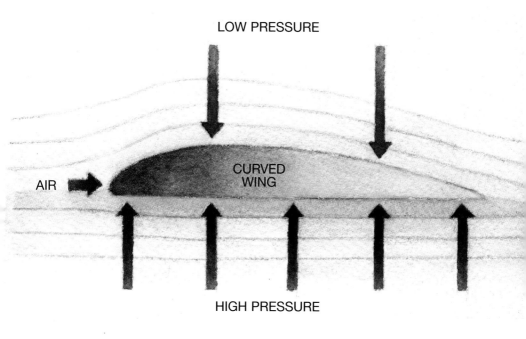

LOW PRESSURE

CURVED WING

AIR

HIGH PRESSURE

Lilienthal had studied lift.

He wanted to see how changing the curve
of a wing would change the lift.

He collected information called data
from his tests.

Then he made charts of the lift data.

Orville and Wilbur could use Lilienthal's charts to build their own glider. But the Wrights would not fly until they knew how to control their machine. They didn't want to crash too. The problem was tricky. Aircraft move in three ways. They turn right or left. That's called yaw. They also tilt side to side. That's called roll. Aircraft move up or down too. That's called pitch. The Wrights had to control all three: yaw, roll, and pitch.

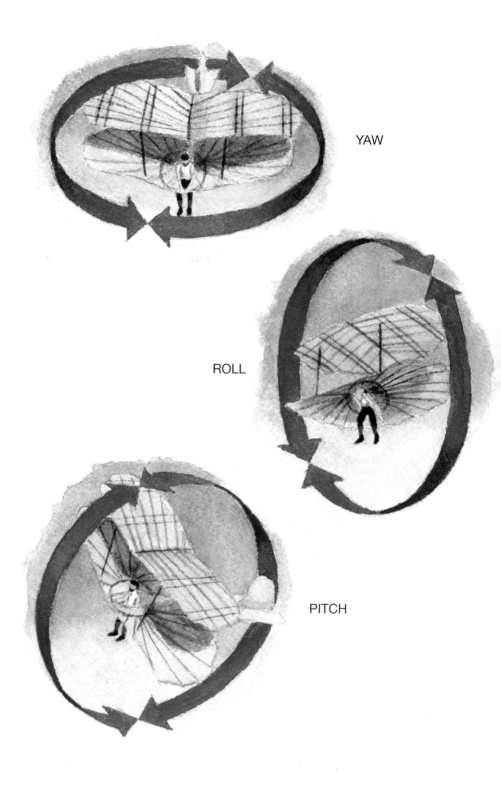

YAW

ROLL

PITCH

Pitch was the easiest to solve.

They could attach a small extra wing
to the front of the glider.

The wing is called an elevator.

The brothers could tilt the wing up and
down with sticks.

This would steer the glider up and down.

The brothers put the elevator in front
for a second reason.
The elevator might protect a pilot in a crash.
The elevator would hit the ground before
the pilot's head would!

After they solved pitch, they thought
about roll.

Could they control the way a glider tilted
from side to side?

They knew that lift pushes up on a wing.

They also knew that changing the shape
of a wing could create more lift.

What if they changed the shape of a wing
on only one end?

Lift would push one end of the wing
higher than the other.

The glider would tilt in the air.

But how could they change the shape of
a wing while the glider was flying?

One day in 1899, Wilbur was fixing
a bicycle tire.
He took an inner tube out of a box.
He twisted the box in his hands.
An idea popped into his head!

Wilbur ran home to show Orville.

He twisted the box.

The long sides changed shape.

One corner pointed up.

Another corner pointed down.

They could build wings
that twisted like the box.

Twisting the wings would change
their shape.

And changing their shape would change lift.

If the lift were greater on one end of the
glider than the other, the glider would tilt.

This idea is called wing warping.

Wilbur built a kite to test his new idea.

He used sticks to tilt the wings
as the kite flew.

The kite tilted just as he had planned.

The test was a success!

INNER TUBE BOX

WING DESIGN

The Giant Kite

The brothers were ready to build a glider.
They planned a wingspan of 18 feet.
To be safe, they would first fly the glider
without a pilot.
They would attach it to ropes, like a kite.
They would need a strong wind
for such a giant kite!
They wrote to the United States
Weather Bureau.
Where could they find a windy place?
The answer came back.
It was Kitty Hawk, North Carolina.

In October 1900, the glider was ready.

Wind gusted off the ocean.

It whipped sand at Wilbur and Orville.

It blew so hard, it lifted the glider

to the end of the ropes.

The glider flew well without a pilot.

Would it carry a person?

Wilbur climbed into the glider.

Once again, the wind lifted the giant kite.

The glider was still held by ropes.

But Wilbur was flying!

For weeks, the brothers practiced
controlling the glider.

Time was running out.

The bicycle shop was waiting for them.

Before they left, they wanted to fly
without ropes.

They wanted to free fly.

The brothers lugged their glider
to Kill Devil Hills.

These high sand dunes were about 4 miles
south of Kitty Hawk.

Wilbur flew off the dunes a dozen times.
It felt like sledding down a snowy hill.
But gliding in the air was more fun.

The Wrights collected data.

They recorded wind speed.

They measured the glider's pull
on the rope.

This told them about the glider's lift.

The data looked odd.

The wind speeds should have created
more lift.
The lift was half as much
as the brothers expected.
What was wrong?
They would have to wait and try again
next year.

Challenges

The bicycle shop wasn't busy in winter.
The brothers had time to work on
another glider.
Longer wings would add lift.
Simpler controls would make piloting
easier.
The 1901 glider was ready by July.
They camped at Kill Devil Hills,
next to the dunes.
But the trip did not go well.
First, it rained.
Then mosquitoes swarmed.
The bugs buzzed and bit the brothers
day and night.

The new glider was wrong too.

The lift was off.

And the new controls were terrible!

At least no one got hurt.

Back home in Dayton, Wilbur and
Orville discussed the problem.
Could Lilienthal's charts be wrong?
The brothers decided to build a machine
to study lift.
The blustery wind at the beach
was hard to measure.
A steady wind would make lift easier
to test.

Wilbur and Orville built a long, wooden
box shaped like a tunnel.
A fan at one end blew air
through the box.
Inside, model wings moved in the wind.
A window gave a view of the tests.

The brothers wrote down lift data
for each wing shape.
They made new charts to replace the ones
made by Lilienthal.
In December, Wilbur and Orville had
enough data to work on the next glider.

The 1902 Glider

The brothers used their new lift charts
to plan a wingspan of 32 feet.
They needed better control of yaw.
So they added a tail to the glider
to help steer right and left.
The tail was made of two long rectangles
called vanes.
They tested their new glider
at Kill Devil Hills.
They finally got the lift they expected.
The wind tunnel tests had worked.
But the brothers ran into trouble
with free flights.
The tail made balancing worse!

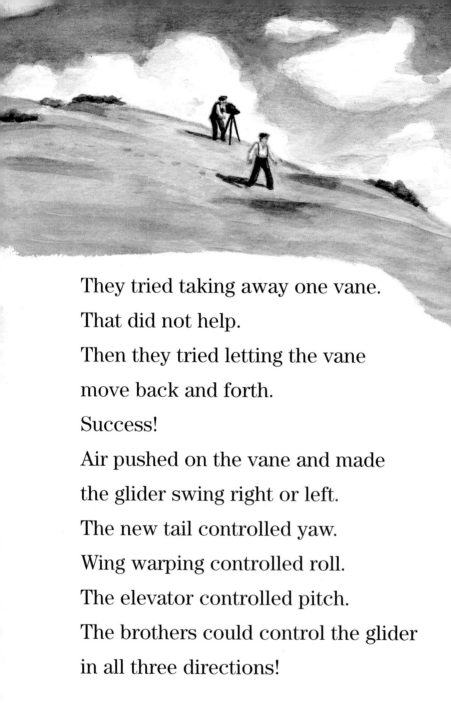

They tried taking away one vane.

That did not help.

Then they tried letting the vane
move back and forth.

Success!

Air pushed on the vane and made
the glider swing right or left.

The new tail controlled yaw.

Wing warping controlled roll.

The elevator controlled pitch.

The brothers could control the glider
in all three directions!

They glided off the sand dunes
almost 800 times.
They flew for fun.
They flew to collect data.
They flew to become better pilots.
And while they flew, they thought.
They thought about a flying machine
that could fly without the wind.

The Flyer

A flying machine that creates
its own power is called an airplane.
How could Wilbur and Orville
make an airplane?
They would need to add an engine
for power.
Propellers would push their airplane
through the air.
But no one made an engine
light enough to fly.
And no one made airplane propellers.
The Wright brothers would have to
build both.

They asked Charlie Taylor to work
on the engine.
Charlie ran the bicycle shop
when the Wrights were away.
They trusted him.
Charlie made the engine
from aluminum to keep it light.
It was perfect.

While Charlie worked, the brothers went
to the library.

Some boats had propellers.

If they read about boat propellers,
maybe they could learn how to make
an airplane propeller.

But no one seemed to know
how propellers worked!

The Wrights went back to their
wind tunnel to study propellers.

They gathered data.

Then they made propellers.

They connected two of them
to Charlie's engine with bicycle chains.

Orville and Wilbur returned
to Kitty Hawk in 1903.
They worked on the new machine.
They called it the Flyer.
But would it fly?
The Flyer could not take off
from soft sand.

The brothers built a 60-foot wooden track
on the sand.
They built a two-wheeled roller
to carry the Flyer.
Wilbur and Orville tossed a coin
to see who would pilot first.
Wilbur won.

He climbed in and got on his stomach.

The motor started.

ROAR!

The propellers turned.

The Flyer moved down the track.

It began to rise into the air.

Oh no!

A gust of wind hit the Flyer.

CRASH!

They had to fix the airplane.

Three days later, they were ready.

On December 17, 1903,

the brothers tried again.

It was Orville's turn.

He climbed into the Flyer.

Wilbur stood beside the airplane.

He held a stopwatch.

Ready?

As soon as the engine started,

the Flyer rolled along the track.

Faster and faster it went.

Then it rose into the air.

The Flyer flew!

Orville landed safely in the sand.

Wilbur's stopwatch showed 12 seconds.

The Flyer had landed 120 feet
from the end of the track.

The brothers made three more flights.

Each time, they flew a little farther.

Then, without warning, a gust of wind
flipped over the Flyer.

The airplane was wrecked.

But the Wrights didn't mind too much.

After all, they had flown the first airplane
in the world.

Just wait until next time. . . .

Afterword

Many inventors dreamt of flying. Why did the Wright brothers succeed? One reason was the way they looked at problems. Wilbur and Orville were curious. They saw problems as a chance to learn. Working step-by-step, they found solutions.

The step-by-step search for knowledge is called the scientific method. There are five steps:

1. State the problem.
2. Brainstorm for solutions.
3. Try a solution.
4. Test the solution and record data.
5. Study the data. Try again, if necessary.

In 1903, the Wrights flew across a beach. Sixty years later, astronauts orbited Earth. Is Mars next? Curiosity and the scientific method make anything possible.

Glossary

air pressure (AIR PRESH-ur): the force of air pushing on a surface

data (DAY-tuh): information learned while testing a machine

elevator (EH-luh-VAY-tur): a small extra wing that is used to steer an aircraft up or down

lift (LIHFT): the force that pushes up on a wing

pitch (PIHTCH): movement of an aircraft up or down

roll (ROHL): movement of an aircraft from side to side

vanes: (VAYNZ): the long rectangles in the tail of the Wright brothers' aircraft

wingspan (WIHNG-span): the length of an aircraft's wings from tip to tip

wing warping (WIHNG WAHR-pihng): twisting wings to steer an aircraft from side to side

yaw (YAW): movement of an aircraft to the right or left

Bibliography

Crouch, Tom D. *The Bishop's Boys: A Life of Wilbur and Orville Wright.* New York: W. W. Norton, 1989.

Crouch, Tom D. *A Dream of Wings: Americans and the Airplane, 1875–1905.* New York: W. W. Norton, 1989.

Jakab, Peter L. *Visions of a Flying Machine: The Wright Brothers and the Process of Invention.* Washington, DC: Smithsonian Institution Press, 1990.

Jeunesse, Gallimard. *Airplanes and Flying Machines.* New York: Scholastic, 1992.

Laboda, Amy. "The Storyteller: NPS Historian Darrell Collins Brings the Wright Brothers Alive." *Sport Aviation,* February 2002: 52–58.

LeCompte, Tom. "The Fifty-Cent Classic." *Air and Space: Smithsonian,* February/March 2002: 20.

Moolman, Valerie. *The Road to Kitty Hawk.* Alexandria, VA: Time-Life Books, 1980.

Moser, Barry. *Fly! A Brief History of Flight Illustrated.* New York: HarperCollins, 1993.

Pallotta, Jerry, and Fred Stillwell. *The Airplane Alphabet Book.* Watertown, MA: Charlesbridge Publishing, 1997.

Potter, Tony. *Planes.* New York: Aladdin Books, 1989.

Schmidt, Norman. *Best Ever Paper Airplanes.* New York: Sterling Publishing Co., 1994.

Smith, Norman F. *Wings of Feathers, Wings of Flame: The Science and Technology of Aviation.* Boston: Little, Brown, 1972.

Willford, Neal. "Airplane Design 101: Six Steps to Designing Your Dream Airplane." *Sport Aviation,* February 2002: 61–68.

Wright, Orville. *How We Invented the Airplane: An Illustrated History.* New York: Dover, 1988.